J

O

S

E

P

H

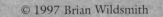

Published jointly 1997
in the United Kingdom by
Oxford University Press
Great Clarendon Street, Oxford OX2 6DP U.K.
and in the United States of America by
Eerdmans Books for Young Readers
an imprint of
Wm. B. Eerdmans Publishing Co.
255 Jefferson Ave. S.E., Grand Rapids, Michigan 49503

Printed in Bahrain

02 01 00 99 98 97   7 6 5 4 3 2 1

Library of Congress Cataloging-in-Publication Data

Wildsmith, Brian.
Joseph / by Brian Wildsmith.
p. cm.
Summary: A retelling of the Old Testament story of Joseph,
whose jealous brothers sold him as a slave into Egypt.
ISBN: 0-8028-5161-4 (cloth: alk. paper)
1. Joseph (Son of Jacob)--Juvenile literature.
2. Bible. O.T. Genesis XXXVII, 1-L, 26--Biography.
3. Bible stories, English--O.T. Genesis.
[1. Joseph (Son of Jacob) 2. Bible stories--O.T.] I. Title.
BS580.J6W546 1997
222'. 11099505--dc21   97-14083
CIP
AC

JOSEPH

Brian Wildsmith

Eerdmans Books for Young Readers

Grand Rapids, Michigan / Cambridge, U.K.

JOSEPH was Jacob's favorite son. Jacob gave Joseph a coat of many colors to show him how much he loved him. Joseph's eleven brothers knew that he was the favorite, and they hated him for it.

One night Joseph had a dream. "Listen," he said to his brothers. "I dreamt that we were all in the field, binding sheaves of grain. My sheaf stood upright, and all your sheaves bowed down to it." The next night he had another dream. "Listen," he said. "I dreamt that the sun and the moon and eleven stars all bowed down to me." Now his brothers hated him even more. "He thinks he is better than us," they said.

Soon a caravan of traders passed by on their way to Egypt. The brothers pulled Joseph out of the pit and sold him to them for twenty pieces of silver. Then they smeared Joseph's coat with goat's blood and took it to their father. "It is Joseph's robe," Jacob said. "A wild beast has torn him to pieces." Jacob was stricken with grief. He wept for many days, and no one could comfort him.

MEANWHILE, the traders took Joseph down to Egypt and sold him in the slave market to Potiphar, captain of Pharaoh's guard.

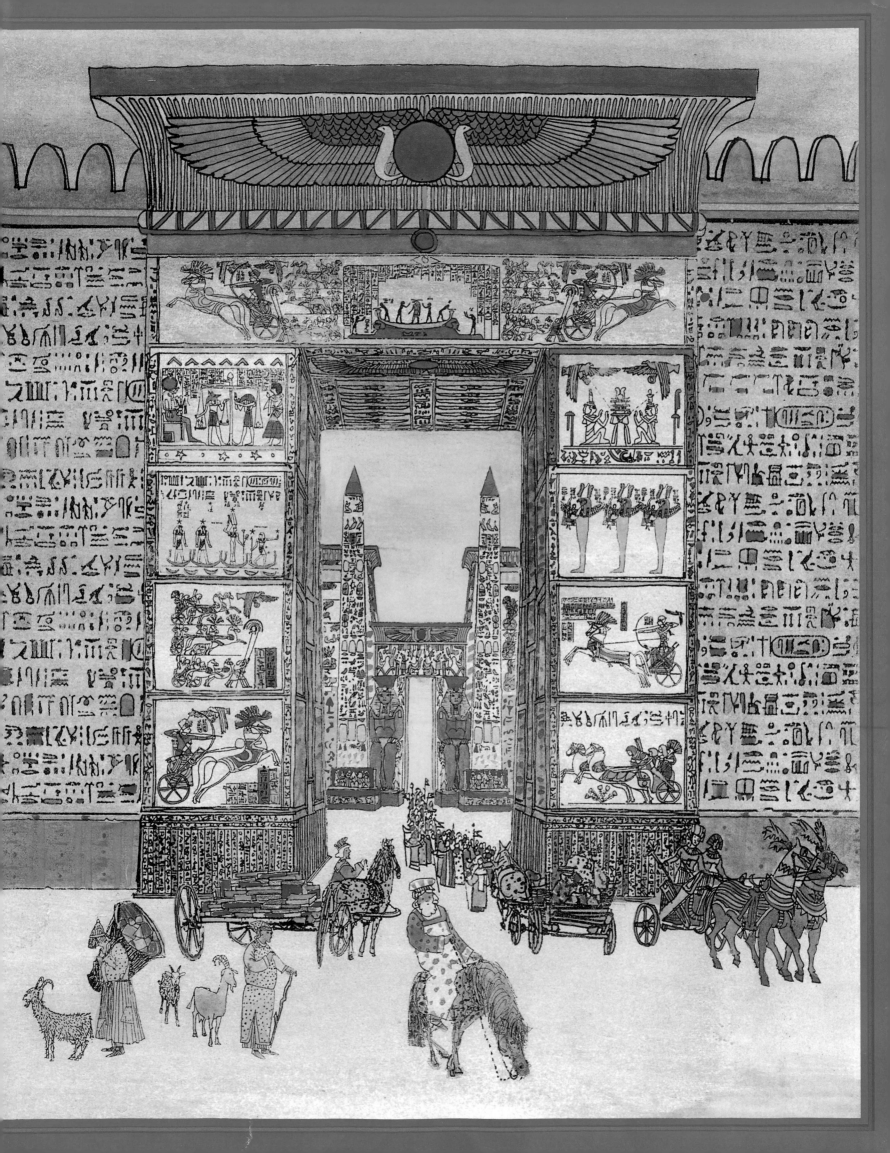

JOSEPH worked so hard for his master that eventually Potiphar put him in charge of all his affairs. By this time, Joseph had grown into a strong and handsome man. Potiphar's wife fell in love with him, and one day she caught Joseph by his cloak and begged him to return her love. But Joseph refused. "How can I betray my master and my God?" he asked her.

Potiphar's wife was furious. She rushed to her husband and accused Joseph of attacking her. Potiphar believed his wife's story and had Joseph thrown into prison.

BUT God was with Joseph in prison. Soon the prison warden put him in charge of all the other prisoners.

One day, according to Pharaoh's orders, two new prisoners arrived: the royal butler and the royal baker. One night, after they both had troubling dreams, they asked Joseph to explain their dreams to them. To the butler he said, "In three days you will be called to the palace and given back your old job of chief butler. When this happens, please remember me and ask Pharaoh to set me free." But to the baker he said, "In three days you too will be called back to the palace. But there you will be put to death."

Three days later it was Pharaoh's birthday. And as Joseph had foretold, the butler was restored to Pharaoh's service, and the baker was put to death. But the butler did not remember Joseph. He forgot all about him.

IT was two years later when Pharaoh himself had disturbing dreams. In the first dream, he was standing by the River Nile when he saw seven fat cows come out of the river. Seven thin cows followed and ate up the fat cows—and then Pharaoh woke up.

He went back to sleep and dreamed again. This time he saw seven fat ears of grain growing on one stalk. Then seven thin ears of grain sprouted up and swallowed the seven fat ears.

When morning came, Pharaoh was very troubled. He sent for all the magicians and wise men of Egypt, but none of them could explain the dreams.

Then the butler remembered Joseph and went to see Pharaoh.

PHARAOH ordered Joseph to be brought out of prison, and he told Joseph his dreams.

"God has revealed what he is about to do," Joseph said. "Both dreams are saying the same thing. There will be seven years of rich harvests, followed by seven years of famine. You must act at once. Appoint a wise man to collect one-fifth of all the grain grown during the seven rich years and store it for the time when the famine comes."

Pharaoh replied, "Since God has revealed all this to you, it is clear that you are the man we need." So Joseph was made Governor of all Egypt, second in power only to Pharaoh himself.

DURING the seven years of rich harvests, Joseph went throughout the land of Egypt. In every city he ordered huge storehouses to be built to hold the surplus grain.

And then, after seven years, the harvests failed, and famine came.
People from all lands traveled to Egypt to buy grain from Joseph.

THE famine spread to the land where Jacob and his family lived. Jacob sent all his sons, except Benjamin, the youngest, down to Egypt to buy grain.

When they came before Joseph, he recognized them, but they had no idea who he was. He treated them like strangers and acted suspicious of them. "You are all spies," he said, and he had them thrown into prison. Three days later he sent for them. "To show me that you really are honest men," he said, "one of you must remain here as a hostage. The rest of you can go home with the food you buy. But you must bring your youngest brother back here to me." The brothers agreed, and Joseph took Simeon as a hostage.

But Joseph played a trick on his brothers. He gave secret orders for the money they had paid for the grain to be put back into their grain sacks.

THE brothers loaded their donkeys and began the journey home to Jacob. But when they arrived, they opened their sacks and discovered their money inside. They were very frightened.

They told their father about everything, including Joseph's demand that they return with Benjamin. Jacob was furious. "You are robbing me of all my children," he said. "Joseph is dead. Simeon is a hostage, and now you want to take Benjamin from me." Jacob refused to let Benjamin go.

AS time went by, the famine grew worse, and all the food the brothers
had brought from Egypt was gone. Jacob called his sons and told them,
"Go back to Egypt and buy more grain."

"But we can't," they reminded him. "Not unless we take Benjamin back with us."

Jacob was very unhappy, but at last he gave in. "Go, and may God protect you," he said. And so the brothers set off for Egypt with Benjamin.

WHEN the brothers arrived in Egypt and presented themselves to Joseph, he had them brought to his house. They were afraid, but he reassured them. He brought Simeon back to them, and he had his steward give them water to wash with, and food for their donkeys. Joseph also ordered a great feast to be prepared.

When Joseph arrived at the feast and saw Benjamin, he nearly burst into tears. "Is this your youngest brother?" he asked. "May God protect him." When the food was served, Benjamin was given five times as much as anyone else.

AFTER the feast, Joseph gave secret orders to his steward. "Fill the men's sacks with food and hide my silver cup in the youngest brother's sack." And early the next day, after the brothers had set off for home, Joseph sent one of his officers to catch up with them. "Somebody has stolen my lord's silver cup!" he shouted.

"No," said the brothers. "If you find the cup in any man's sack, then let him die." And of course the officer searched and found the cup in Benjamin's sack. The brothers, terrified, begged for Benjamin's life. But they were all arrested and taken back to the city.

WHEN Joseph's brothers were brought before him, he pretended to be very angry. "The man who has stolen my cup shall be my slave for life," he said.

But one of the brothers, called Judah, knelt down before Joseph. "Take me as your slave, but not Benjamin," he pleaded. "My father is an old man. One of his beloved sons is dead. And Benjamin is now his favorite son. Have mercy."

Then Joseph could pretend no longer. "I am your brother Joseph whom you sold as a slave," he told them. "But I forgive you. God protected me and sent me here to save all our lives. Now go and bring my father and all his family to live here."

Joseph embraced all his brothers, and they wept for joy together.

AFTER Joseph gave his brothers generous supplies and many gifts, they returned to Jacob to tell him the news.

"Joseph!" said Jacob. "My son Joseph is still alive! I will go to see him before I die." And Jacob set off for Egypt with all his family and possessions.

When Jacob was still on his way, Joseph went out to meet his father and knelt before him. "It is enough," said Jacob. "I have seen your face and know that you are still alive."

PHARAOH, King of Egypt, sailed down the River Nile on his golden barge to welcome Joseph's father. "I offer you the beautiful land of Goshen," he said, "the best of all the land in Egypt. Here you may stay with all your family."

And so Jacob and his eleven sons and their families settled in
Goshen near Joseph, and lived peacefully there for the rest of
their lives.